Find Your Way
HOME

Find Your Way
HOME
Moving Through Miscarriage

Poems and Practices to
Reclaim Your Light After Loss

VICTORIA MARGAUX NIELSEN

Copyright © 2023 by Victoria Margaux Nielsen

All rights reserved. No part of this publication may be reproduced, distributed or transmitted in any form or by any means without permission of the publisher, except in the case of brief quotations referencing the body of work and in accordance with copyright law.

The information given in this book should not be treated as a substitute for professional medical advice; always consult a medical practitioner. Any use of information in this book is at the reader's discretion and risk. Neither the author nor the publisher can be held responsible for any loss, claim or damage arising out of the use, or misuse, of the suggestions made, the failure to take medical advice or for any material on third party websites.

ISBN 978-1-913590-81-9 Paperback

ISBN 978-1-913590-82-6 Ebook

The Unbound Press
www.theunboundpress.com

Hey unbound one!

Welcome to this magical book brought to you by The Unbound Press.

At The Unbound Press we believe that when women write freely from the fullest expression of who they are, it can't help but activate a feeling of deep connection and transformation in others. When we come together, we become more and we're changing the world, one book at a time!

This book has been carefully crafted by both the contributors and publisher with the intention of inspiring you to move ever more deeply into who you truly are.

We hope that this book helps you to connect with your Unbound Self and that you feel called to pass it on to others who want to live a more fully expressed life.

With much love,
Nicola Humber

Founder of The Unbound Press
www.theunboundpress.com

*To Sebastian, Rocky & Will, you are the reason for it all.
Thank you for choosing me.*

Contents

Foreword	i
My Miscarriage	1
Four Years Later	8
Choosing Joy	10
Connecting With Your Intuition	13
Honoring Your Inner Child	15
Stop Numbing Yourself	18
Leaning Into Gratitude	20
Feel Your Feelings	22
You Are Your Own Medicine	25
Words From the Heart	27
Prompts & Practices	117
Journaling	119
Affirmations	120
Akashic Prayer	122
Oracle Cards	129
Breathwork	129
Dancing	132
Grounding	133
Acknowledgments	135
About the Author	137

Foreword

Here are my words from the heart; musings from a woman, and mama, trying to find herself and her place in this world after losing something sacred.

Since high school, I've used words and journaling to ease the aching of my heart. To express a longing and a deep craving for connection to others. A true tenderness I saved only for the page and rarely shared with anyone else.

As I got older, I forgot about this gift, this companion. As one does. But then, in my late twenties, a miscarriage rocked me to my core. It uprooted a restlessness I'd felt inside for years. A longing that I'd poured into booze, drugs, other people... really anything but myself.

This time, I listened to that inner voice that asked me to pour back into myself instead. The voice that said "surrender." To what, I didn't know. I wasn't a religious person. I didn't pray.

But I found myself naturally falling into my own type of devotion each day. A devotion of self. A devotion of trust. A devotion of love.

Little by little, I crawled out of the hole of grief to find that I'd completely transformed. And that writing and sharing words from the heart had helped me do that.

Now, a healthy son and second baby on the way later, I find words pouring from my soul again. Instead of grief, they are words of power and love. Of encouragement. Of courageousness. Of fearlessness.

They're words I know I needed at some point in my life, and I hope they're what you need, too. A balm to your soul when you crave them most. A precious gift from my guides, angels, and higher self. To be read over and over, dog-eared and shared. The light that guides you in the dark.

I hope you feel the vibration of every single word in this piece. To me, it's a piece. A dance. A tango. A weaving. Just as in life, I am co-creating this dance with my heart, the essence of this book, and the story it wants to tell.

Some of these poems are from so long ago, I'm a whole different person than the woman who wrote them. Others came to me just yesterday. This is the journey I've been on the last four years. The ups, the downs, the void in between. I'm holding nothing back from you, dear reader, in the hope that you know you can do the same. You can show your vulnerability to the world, you can let people in. It isn't a burden or something to be ashamed of. Our feelings are our magic in this world. Our experiences are what connect us. You are not alone.

My wish for you is that these words move you to feel something. That they open a portal to your heart, to that little girl inside who maybe felt unloved, or uncared for. That your reading of this work is a beautiful exchange of energy. Filling in some of the holes you didn't even know you had inside. Let's fill them with light. Let's fill them with love.

I want to show you that miscarriage, or anything tragic that happens to you, doesn't have to define you. I want to show you that all parts of you are beautiful — especially the messy ones.

I want to share a woman in all of her stages. In all of her facets. In all of her glory. Every single part of what makes her unique, and the many feelings she can vacillate between on a daily basis — shameful, sad, weary, bubbly, bright-eyed, and the full spectrum in between. This piece is all of my facets laid to paper. May I be a mirror for all of the beautiful facets inside of you.

No matter where you are on your journey, I hope these words light a spark in you where maybe there was only darkness. A flicker of flame where you previously stood barren. My light is your light. I am no different than you. I am no better.

I am. And so are you. We are limitless.

I love you,
Victoria

My Miscarriage

It started with three words I'll never forget: "There's no heartbeat."

There were no warning signs. No blood. No dramatic movie moment. Just there one minute and gone the next. With those three little words, it was like my life split in two. Before we lost the baby, and then after.

We'd had a perfectly normal early ultrasound at six weeks because we were traveling abroad. That little blip was there on the monitor, just minding its own business, and we didn't think anything of it. Of course, we were grateful, but we didn't know we had anything to be extra-grateful for. We completely took its beautiful existence for granted.

We may have heard the sound of his heartbeat, but I honestly don't remember. (I say "his" because I feel like it was a boy, but he never made it far enough along to confirm either way.) I didn't know we'd never hear it again. The thought of it not being there at our next appointment never crossed our minds. Never. Not even for an instant. We packed our bags and were visiting Turkey by the end of the week.

Back from our trip and ready to see our baby, our next appointment was scheduled for nine weeks. Because I didn't have any bleeding, cramping, or signs of distress at all, when the doctor couldn't find the heartbeat with the handheld doppler, I thought maybe the baby was just in a weird position. Even when she calmly shepherded us to the ultrasound room, it felt totally normal.

When my OB silently looked at the unmoving screen, I still didn't think anything could be wrong. There's not much to see at that point anyway, right? The cells still look like a blob.

Then, she turned to us and uttered those three words, adding an "I'm sorry" at the end like it would lessen the blow. I think I said, "Huh?" or "What?" or some other disclaimer of disbelief, and finally burst into tears when she had to repeat it.

Shocked doesn't feel like a big enough word to encapsulate how I felt. We were totally blindsided. Based on its size, the baby had stopped growing a week or two prior. A week or two where I was blissfully unaware that I was no longer going to be a mama in seven months.

I had to have a D&C procedure, and although I remember everyone at the facility being extremely kind, I don't remember much else beyond the bright lights of the operating room before I was put to sleep.

Waking up the next day was the strangest feeling. I started to cradle my stomach instinctively, only to have to remind myself there was no longer a baby in there. That felt more surreal than the day the doctor broke the news. I still felt pregnant. My belly was still pooched, my boobs still felt sore. It's like my body hadn't gotten the heartbreaking memo.

I vacillated between being sad and angry all day. I stayed in bed and cried and didn't want to talk to anyone. My best friend sent flowers and I wanted to throw them off the fucking porch. I remember thinking flowers were for the dead and nothing had died here… but it had.

Days kept moving by and life kept continuing on, but there was nothing outside of me to mark the change. Nothing that said I was changed, because I was, and profoundly. I desperately wanted something, anything to feel different. So, I did what any woman would do: I dyed my hair.

It didn't last long. I chose to dye my rich, dark brown hair grey (note to self: dark hair doesn't hold pigment like that very well), and pretty soon, it just looked like I'd tried to dye my ends an unflattering brassy blonde. That's when I knew I needed to do more than just something superficial. I needed to shift internally, as well.

I vividly remember falling to my knees outside my bedroom door weeks later, saying, "I surrender, I surrender," in between loud sobs, pressing my forehead to the floor. To what I was surrendering, I really didn't know. I just wanted to let something higher than myself take the wheel. I wanted to stop feeling the waves of grief so acutely. I wanted to heal, and this felt like a Hail Mary when I didn't know what else to do.

Nothing else had allowed me to feel fully held and supported. Nothing else had returned me to any semblance of normalcy. I kept finding myself at the bottom of the well of grief again and again, and I wanted a way out. I wanted to believe that things could be good again. I wanted to feel less alone and let some light into the neverending darkness.

Because when all I could do was surrender and give myself over to a higher power, I had to start trusting that things would work out. I had to put my trust in the everyday actions that were moving me forward.

I'd been journaling daily, and even tried to meditate for the first time, but it felt like a band-aid on a geyser of a wound. That's when I started following the nudges from the universe and found the Akashic Records.

What are the Akashic Records? The Records are an energetic frequency and higher perspective absolutely anyone can use to tap into their divine masters, teachers, and loved ones on a regular basis for the exact guidance needed in the moment.

I could honestly write a whole book about the Records — they're my favorite tool of healing and empowerment — but for the sake of not getting sidetracked, I'll save the most important details for the practice at the back of this book. If you're itching to learn more, skip to page 122 and come back.

After hearing about the Records on a podcast, continuously pulling the "Akasha" oracle card, and getting a reading with the woman who would ultimately become my teacher, I couldn't ignore the pull. This was something I was supposed to learn how to do.

It wasn't a coincidence my teacher, Daniela Gil, had a training starting the very next week. I'd never done anything remotely like this before — even getting an Akashic reading was kind of far-fetched for me at the time — but it felt like something my soul was yearning to explore. And if it was as peaceful as the energy I experienced during my reading, I was all for giving it a try. I've always enjoyed learning new things, and it gave me something to look forward to twice a week.

I started opening my Akashic Record almost daily after that, and the feeling of being wrapped in a warm hug was the only thing that kept me going some days. The energy made me feel lighter, while the messages that I was loved and it was all going to be okay were exactly what I needed.

And the more I surrendered to the Records and my inner voice within, the more I realized I was one and the same with this energy. I was the Records and the Records were me. I was connected to this universal life-force energy, just as you are, just as we're all connected to every living thing on this planet.

I would say that was the "official" start of my spiritual journey, even though I wouldn't call it that just yet.

The Akashic Records ultimately confirmed I was pregnant again before a blood test even did. After my period didn't return regularly four months post-miscarriage, I went back to the doctor. She put me on a round of progesterone to hopefully force my period and was going to start me on another round when I told her "no" and listened to my intuition instead.

At that point, I'd already done a blood test — that came back negative — because I believed so strongly that I was pregnant again. Finally, a pregnancy test came back positive, and we found out I was nine weeks along. I'm grateful we found out more than two months in, but it didn't stop me from being a ball of anxiety the entire pregnancy.

Every appointment, I held my breath, praying the heartbeat would pick up on the doppler. Every appointment, my blood pressure was elevated at the office. Eventually, I made peace with my anxious thoughts using some of the prompts and practices at the back of this book, and you can, too. I'm proof you can have a healthy pregnancy (or two!) after miscarriage.

Four Years Later

Now, I know how common miscarriages are (according to the National Library of Medicine, it's as high as 1 in 4 pregnancies), but at the time, I didn't think I even knew anybody who'd had one. Sharing my experience when I was ready allowed me to see how untrue that really was. So many women came forward with similar stories (some with multiple). All of them went on to have healthy babies.

It may be horrible to say, but I often don't think about my miscarriage at all now. Then, it felt like a cleaving. Everything I thought I knew about my body, my faith in life, how things would unfold. Shattered in an instant.

And although my journey started with a miscarriage, it doesn't define it. It doesn't define me. It was the catalyst I needed to awaken. To question. To blossom. To stop numbing myself to life and really live it instead. I believe wholeheartedly things couldn't have happened any other way.

I wrestled with making this book one about miscarriage because it really feels like it happened to a whole different person. That's how far I've come. But then I realized that's why I should. I've overcome one of the most devastating things you can experience as a woman — and you can, too. You can overcome anything that's happened to you.

To be clear, this doesn't diminish any grief you may still feel for yours if you've experienced one (or several). Or whatever part of YOUR healing journey you're still on. If I've learned anything over these last few years, it's that each person is on their own unique journey, and mine is just one perspective of many. It's a sad moment that had a happy ending.

Choosing Joy

Ultimately, I chose joy instead. I chose to let this heart-shattering event truly break me wide open, so I could see the real me at my core. The me that can't be put in a box or labeled one particular thing. The me I'd always been before the world told me who I should be. I thought I knew, but as I peeled back the layers, I realized there were so many sides of myself I had yet to explore (and am still exploring).

I chose me. I chose that little girl at my core who is free, and open, and full of joy. Because joy is a choice. One you sometimes have to claw your way back to. Other days, it may not feel like a choice at all (that's always the dream, right?), but walking the path of light doesn't mean everything is given to you. It's work. It's uncomfortable. I don't believe it means sacrifice. Selflessness maybe. But not sacrifice.

I am more "me" now than I ever was before my miscarriage. And it starts with the small steps I took every day to connect inward and heal. To shed. To release. Did I let myself wallow? Yes. Did I get angry? Absolutely. Some of the words you'll read next reflect that, but I didn't let myself stay there. I chose to rise again and again — even on the days I didn't want to.

Allow these words to be an activation for you to rise — no matter what you're going through — and know that it won't always be hard. It won't always feel like you're swimming through the static.

There were days I felt real gratitude in the months that followed my miscarriage. And other days, I felt like I was drowning. All I could do was take it a day at a time. Open my eyes. Meditate or roll out my yoga mat. Grab my journal. Write until I felt like I'd released what I needed to. Go to work. Repeat.

There's no magic formula for moving through a life-changing event — even if it's a good one. Returning to myself, and ultimately what I found to be my intuition and inner child, every single day was the thread that helped me through the darkness.

My yoga practice, my body, and my surrender to something higher than myself allowed me to see there was never any other choice for me. I was always going to rise again. I was always going to choose to live and love fiercely. And once the floodgates were open, there was no going back.

Once you start to feel, and feel deeply, you realize all the ways in which you weren't before. All the things you weren't paying attention to because you were rushing around checking things off a to-do list or "living" by escaping into distractions all around you.

When you're stuck in your own cycle of numbness, it's much harder to get out and see how joyful life already is. You have to want to get out. And I know that's hard some days. I know that joy can feel like a burden at first — especially when feeling any type of emotion is already so much for your broken heart.

But little by little, moment by moment, as you choose clarity over not feeling, you'll realize it gets better. As you open yourself up to guidance from the universe, the gentle nudges and signs of your intuition start to appear louder, brighter, more vibrant, less easily ignored.

Sure, feeling ALL things means you feel the bad things, too. But that's what makes the good things sweeter. And that's what allows you to realize you have support as you navigate the ups and downs of life. You aren't alone. You were never alone. When you allow yourself to be guided by the universe, the messages will come in loud and clear.

Connecting With Your Intuition

My way through the hard days was getting on my yoga mat every morning to stretch, dance, and move in whatever way my body felt called to. To give reverence to myself and my divine form. Even though I felt like my body had failed me, reconnecting to it every day allowed me to forgive and see its strength. It may no longer be carrying a baby, but it was carrying me. When I started doing it every single day without fail, I began to see signs from the universe, little nudges that there was light at the end of this tunnel of grief.

I should tell you, signs are subtle. We often want them to be blazing neon road signs pointing us in the exact direction we're meant to go, but the universe doesn't work like that. We have free will. WE have to choose to follow the path. WE have to choose the red pill.

The way your intuition speaks to you is a deeply personal thing. One you have to figure out and cultivate over time. You're unique and so is how the universe connects to you.

It's a relationship that takes watering and getting to know. And the more you listen, the more the signs become apparent.

I often find signs in nature, and even just being outside for five minutes can allow me to reset and tap in to that higher connection. I can always discover a hello from the universe — a moth, a grasshopper, a bumblebee — to remind me that I'm not alone when I'm overwhelmed. Nature is also just extremely calming to the nervous system.

Honoring Your Inner Child

I used to spend hours laying in the grass of my grandmother's backyard when I was little, and I found myself doing it again as I continued to connect with the little girl inside who felt so alone after losing both the baby *and* herself.

We all have a little child inside of us that is yearning for love, for the emotions and care we maybe didn't experience growing up or don't receive in our current life on a regular basis. As adults, we stifle this inner-child-like part of us that craves simple pleasures — the wind on her face, her feet in the grass — or to dance and sing with wild abandon. To me, tapping into my inner child means I'm perfectly present with myself and what's happening in my surroundings. It allows me to drop into moments of play at any given time, and not stay trapped in the never-ending loop that is my brain some days.

When I'm *really* honoring my inner child, I find synchronicities abound. Things like Angel Numbers —

repeating digits — on the clock began appearing almost daily during this time. 1111 was a favorite. Our house was even numbered 1111, and I'd always believed it was an auspicious sign. Seeing it, again and again, was a form of validation for me to keep going. To keep doing what I was doing. Putting one foot in front of the other every day, even if I didn't know how or when I'd eventually feel better.

All I could do was return to that little girl inside who felt broken, who felt like her body had betrayed her, and wrap her up tight in my arms, giving her unconditional love. It's easy to want to punish yourself, to feel like you did something wrong that caused this terrible thing to happen.

I'm here to tell you: you didn't.

When I remembered little Victoria was ultimately who I was talking to, who I was returning to, it was hard to stay mad at her. She was so innocent. It allowed me to see that I was innocent, too. I didn't do anything wrong. I didn't fail. This soul just wasn't ready to come Earthside yet, and I had a journey to go on so that I could be a better mother and human being when they did decide to come.

Our babies choose us for a reason, just as we chose our parents. We made soul contracts with them before coming to Earth with all the lessons we wanted to learn together and the karma we wanted to clear.

Now that doesn't mean we get to pick the *exact* circumstances we experience — it doesn't work like that — but it does all work for your highest good and highest alignment, even if it feels like the exact opposite in the moment.

Stop Numbing Yourself

If you're numbing yourself, as we so often do when swallowed in grief, it's so easy to miss the subtle signs from the universe to keep going. The cardinal outside your window, the rose on your way to work, the song playing on the radio.

There are so many ways to numb ourselves to the world. It doesn't have to be with a substance. Do you constantly pick up your phone and scroll to keep yourself "engaged" because just sitting doing nothing makes your mind freak out? I've been there. And I've found the more you get sucked into the cycle of picking up your phone, the more you want to do it. It's like a drug in and of itself.

Breaking the cycle of chaos isn't done overnight. I say chaos because that's what my mind feels like when I'm constantly distracting myself. When I find myself in this state of hyperarousal, even I sometimes avoid doing the things I know I need to — putting the phone down and taking deep breaths. Even just three minutes of deep breathing can completely alter my mindset to one of calmness, focus, and clarity. I share some of my favorite breathwork practices starting on page 129.

During the height of my grief, I stopped picking up my phone first thing in the morning and started journaling instead. My yoga mat became a trusted friend I could take my frustrations out on after crawling out of bed. Or I'd read a few pages of a book like this one, books filled with poems that made me feel less alone and put words to the tumultuousness inside I was at a loss for how to explain.

Leaning Into Gratitude

Gratitude was another tool I turned to often to try and focus on the good during the days that felt anything but. I made lists and lists of the things I was thankful for. Some days, the only thing I could find was that I'd opened my eyes, that my lungs were pumping air through my body, that my feet worked. Other days, I was able to profoundly shift my energy. And although my heart still hurt, it was a lot more at peace.

My D&C happened right before Christmas, and I wanted nothing more than to curl up and be left alone. But we'd already made plans, so instead, we visited family. I balked at the idea when my husband said it would make me feel better. I was still bleeding while everyone else was in high spirits for the holidays. Why the fuck would I want to be around other people right now?

I wasn't my normal self, of course, but there was one day I really didn't want to get out of bed. I pulled the covers over my head, curled into a fetal position, and cried at the thought of having to even interact with another human.

After a few deep breaths, I grabbed my journal and started methodically moving through each person in the house, pausing to reflect: "I am grateful for [insert person here] because…." Before I knew it, I'd filled the entire page. It surprised me when I started tearing up again, but not because I was sad. Because it was the first time I felt connected and thankful since it'd happened. It shifted my mood enough that I could see a new perspective.

And that's all you need sometimes. A perspective shift. A little nudge. For me, gratitude was the missing link. Because I really was grateful. I already had so much. And allowing myself a glimmer of that positivity led to hope and genuine feeling. It was profound.

I actually ended up writing some of my favorite words that morning, tucked away in a guest room by myself. Mercifully, everyone gave me a wide berth on that trip, and writing my gratitude list allowed me to be grateful for that kindness, too.

Feel Your Feelings

Being present, really and truly present, has a way of making everything else fall away — that bone-weary ache that you're carrying, the worry, and the racing thoughts. When you focus your whole attention on something, one thing at a time, there isn't room for anything else. And then your soul starts to speak and the healing begins.

Instead of searching for the next distraction, allow yourself to just be exactly as you are in this moment. Don't try to change it, alter it, or avoid it. Let whatever is rising within you begin to rise. For it's in these moments that we're able to see our true selves. We are not our feelings, but they have important messages for us around what we're longing for, mourning, craving, or working towards.

Your feelings are your compass pointing you out of the haze. Through *anything* you're currently experiencing. The only way out is through.

Those sensations in your body? That ickiness in your chest or the unease you feel deep down in your belly? They're feelings trying to surface. Don't ignore them. Don't push them down. Let them be.

Instead, get comfortable with observing your thoughts and feelings. And then go beyond them. What are they trying to tell you? What truths are trying to come to light? Lean in. Go deeper.

Feeling everything fully is what allows you to choose how you want to move forward. I made a conscious choice after my miscarriage to feel every second of it. I didn't numb myself with booze or other substances. I didn't try to escape. And that's what freed me in the end. That's what allowed me to start healing.

Whatever compelled you to pick up this book —motherhood, a soul-shaking tragedy, just navigating everyday life — it won't last forever. This is just a moment in time, and the feelings and emotions you're experiencing are fleeting. I know it might not feel like it right now, but before you know it, you'll be in a different season of your life.

One day, you'll wake up and it won't hurt so much. You may even go the whole morning without thinking about it. Then the whole day, then a whole week will pass by. Until one day, you'll have to remind yourself that you were ever sad for days on end. And then you might even feel guilty for not feeling as sad as you once did. It's all okay. It's all welcome here.

That might seem unimaginable to you now, but I promise you it *will* happen. The mind has a way of protecting us. Of blurring things around the edges until we don't remember them being as terrible as they once were. It doesn't mean it won't still hurt in waves, or that you've forgotten. Instead, you've learned to live with it. To grow around it. To be one with the experience.

And then you'll be ready to try again, and you'll hold your breath every month as you wait to see if your period comes. It can be excruciating if you let it. Don't.

This is where I should probably share some trope about it being "worth the wait" or "all in divine time." Instead, I'm going to say it's okay to be impatient. It's okay to get anxious. It's okay to get frustrated it's not happening fast enough. You're human. You're not a robot. I'd be worried if you didn't feel these things.

But don't bottle them up. Channel these feelings into healthy avenues. This is where that surrender comes back in.

You'll hopefully get pregnant again, but there will be a little pebble of fear that sits in the pit of your belly. What if it happens again? I'm here to ask you: So what if it does? You'll deal with it then, too. There's no sense in future-tripping about something that hasn't happened yet. It's only going to bring you anxiety. And it might actually mean you aren't ready to move on just yet, and that's 1,000% okay. I'm here to tell you that statistics are on your side and that anything is possible. Truly.

You Are Your Own Medicine

No matter how you choose to navigate these tumultuous waters, I want you to know one important thing: you are your own medicine. You are your own healer and wise woman. You have everything you need inside of you to feel better and rise again.

As I said earlier, I'm a whole different person than the woman who had a miscarriage four years ago. And that's a good thing. It sent me on such a journey of self-discovery that I only leaned into deeper after having my boys. It also allowed me to really see how fragile life is. How much of a miracle I am. It took so much for me to even be born. All of the chance encounters that had to happen so my great great great x 12 grandparents could meet and then eventually have me.

The same goes for you. You wouldn't be here if all the people who came before you hadn't met, and loved, and lost, and lived.

Miscarriage doesn't have to define you. YOU get to define you. You get to choose who you become every second of every day. A spiritual journey — because let's be honest, this *is* a spiritual journey, even if you don't necessarily connect with that word — isn't about finding what was lost, but rather it's about excavating what you already have within. Chiseling away at all the labels and feelings others and society have placed on you, so YOU get to decide who you want to be.

And if that person is different from the woman who woke up yesterday? Amazing! You'll get to know new parts of yourself you didn't even know existed. Follow dreams that you didn't even know were yours. You can create a whole new version of yourself any time you like. Lean into the fire, lean into the journey. Who knows who you'll be on the other side?

You may wander
You may forget
But you can always come home
To your body
To your breath
To yourself.

I'm sending love to all the mamas, soon-to-be mamas, not-quite-yet mamas, hopeful mamas and all the mamas in-between. I'm here with you, and I love you.

words from the heart

I am more than a mother.

I am more than a wife.

I am more than a friend.

I am more than a sister.

I am more than a goddess.

I am more than a daughter.

I am more than a human.

I am more than the side of myself you are used to.

I am more than the side of myself you see.

I am more than the side of myself you want to keep in a box.

I am more than the side of myself you think you can label.

I am more than any one side of myself.

I am more than the sum of my parts.

I am more than any label you can put on me.

I am more than.

I am.

Me.

If only you knew how divinely you were held.

If only you knew how all of the specks of the universe had to combine in your favor.

If only you knew how uniquely designed you are, god's gift to Earth.

If only you knew that high you're chasing won't last.

If only you knew that the love you're so desperately seeking can only come from yourself.

If only you knew that a stomach gorged on food won't fill the hole you feel inside.

If only you knew that you are so loved and cherished, exactly as you are.

If only you knew angels wept and the sun shone bright on the day you were born.

If only you knew your tears were floods of excess energy leaving their bright trails down your face.

If only you knew that you didn't need all of those fake friends, the booze or the drugs.

If only you knew the searching and the fear you felt were of your own choosing.

If only you knew.

You can do this
You can be this
You can make friends with your fear
You can make friends with the voices
The ones that tell you that you aren't worthy
That you can't
That you should stay small

Love them
Caress them
Allow them in so that you can show them the way
So you can show them love

You are a magnet for miracles
Delicious miracles
You weren't born to stay small
You were put here to thrive
To live
To love
To give

Honor yourself
Honor this mission from god
It's a worthy one
Because you are worthy
Even on the days you don't feel like you are
Even on the days you do absolutely nothing at all

You don't have to do anything to deserve love
You are worthy of it exactly as you are
Drink in that feeling

Drink in that acceptance
That peace
It's yours for the taking
It's yours to claim
So claim it
Be it
You are it

It's okay to be happy again.

It's okay to move forward with grace.

It's okay to smile and love and laugh.

You aren't meant to stay sad forever.

It isn't a betrayal to hope again.

You'll never forget, even when the world wants you to.

A mother never does.

But don't let it be an anchor that pulls you down, down, down.

Let it be an anchor that steadies you, like your heart.

To your soul, to your purpose, to your truth.

To the never-ending love you have for your baby.

Let it multiply like butterfly wings.

Sending love from flower to flower, allowing you to bloom again.

I release the sorrow and shame

Every time you say my name

It's a prayer

It's a gift

I am, I am, I am

I release any stagnation

Release the trauma and the shame

Know my name

I am in the wind

I am in the trees

I am in all things

I am in you

Just as you are in me

I release this mortal body, this bag of bones

It feels like stones

I will not drown

I will fly

I will touch the sky

I will spread my wings and soar so high

So high

I am a bird

I am an eagle

I am a child's eye

I am all things

Why do we run away from the things we need?
Because we're afraid they'll reveal ourselves to us, and we won't like what we see.
We won't like the truth staring us so boldly in the face we don't have any other choice but to listen
To change
To grow
To evolve
To look the elephant in the room in the eye and kindly ask it to leave.

Change asks us to be a different, better version of ourselves.
And it's scary
And daunting
And sometimes we don't feel up to the challenge
Because we don't believe we deserve better.
Deep down, we don't think we're worthy of anything else beyond what we already have.

If we could give ourselves exactly what we needed in the moment, we'd see we actually don't need the external stuff around us.
The relationship
The job
The fancy things.

And then what are we without those things?
100% ourselves
And what if we don't measure up?
What if living as us, living from our heart's desires, brings us heartache?

Maybe it will. But it absolutely will if you continue to live as someone else. For someone else.

You'll become a shell of yourself
A self-fulfilling prophecy not living up to your full potential.

I am deeply safe and supported.
I am open to receive.
Like a tree with its leaves gently reaching toward the sun.
I receive love.
I receive light.
I receive absolutely everything I need.
I receive.

I am grounded.
I am safe.
I am secure.
I am.

All of my cells are smiling.
Grateful for this life.
For this moment.
For this breath.
For the life I'll bring into this world.
And for the lives that I get to touch every single day.
I LOVE MY LIFE.

Repeat this daily:

May all the dark places inside of me be lightened with love.
May all my nooks and crannies be filled with joy.
I am living my highest timeline now.
I am abundant.
I am prosperous.
I am taking aligned action every moment of every day.

Don't bury the grief too deep, my child,
For your soul will weep
Don't bury the grief too deep, my child or the Earth won't sleep
Let it live in your bones and in your skin
Let it sink in
Let it become one with you, and you with it
Traveling through your marrow and into your core
Not buried, no, but forever more
Flowing through you, as lucid as the sun
Let it flow through you, as we've only just begun
This isn't the first and it won't be the last
Your heart is meant for this, feel it as it beats fast
Pumping your blood, your memories, and so much more
Feel the sorrow, feel it deep in your core
Watch as it turns into a stone so blue
Carry it inside you, carry it through
Around it, you weave all the memories and feelings and thoughts
Forming a protective web of the finest gold thread
Take it out and look at it, whenever you must
But it's a part of you now and so you must trust
Trust

Open your eyes and truly see.

Your magic abounds.

And it talks to the birds and the bees.

It's carried from flower to flower on butterfly's wings.

You are a ripple in time.

You create waves with your emotions.

With your feelings.

With your force.

Although you be mighty, be gentle.

The littlest movement still has a profound effect.

Why do you feel as though you are unworthy?
You are made of God, and one of God's children.
So you are infinitely worthy.

We are all made in God's image
And so we are infinitely worthy by just being
By breathing
By experiencing
What events in your life have made you feel small?
Now is the time to forgive them. Those people. Those places. Those things.
They don't hold any sway over you anymore.
Let it go, let it go, let it go
It's not serving you anymore
It's not meant to come forward with you into this next version of yourself
The lighter, brighter version of you that is unfolding
With each release, you become more free
Of the shackles you've placed upon yourself to keep you small
Because you're afraid of being seen, really seen.
Somewhere along the way, you started to feel unwanted
But that's not true
It's just a story you told yourself
It's just a reflection of others' perceptions
Not your own
You know you are mighty
And worthy
And oh so loved
Drink it in
Believe it
It's no trick

It's the truth
You deserve all the happy and good things
We all do
It's time to start believing it

For you are made of the same salt, and the same water
The same rising and falling
Of the tides
Of your emotions
Of the waves & depths of your soul

Let her love lull you
Let it fill you
All the nooks and crannies
So that you may be at peace once more
Thank you for this miracle

May you keep making waves
No matter how big or small
Your presence has a ripple effect
You matter
Your energy matters

Put down what you are carrying

A sacred release
A river of tears
A baptism in your own salt and sadness
That ultimately leads to renewal
To a washing away of whatever wasn't meant to be

And each day you let the light fill the cracks a little more.
Sealing over like gold.
Not brand new.
But like you will be.
In time.

Listening takes more than your ears.

Seeing takes more than your eyes.

Feeling takes more than your heart.

Let your guard down.
Let people in.
They can heal as much as they hurt.
Be gentle with yourself.
Forgive yourself.
Love yourself.

TRUST that the path you're walking on is the right one.

TRUST that you are provided and cared for beyond your wildest dreams.

TRUST that any unraveling, breaking, or heartache just means something fell apart so something better could come together.

TRUST that everything will work out as it should (or even better than you could have imagined).

TRUST in the power of your inner knowing to show you the way.

There's a crack in your facade
But it's to let more love in
The clouds are clearing and the path is becoming clear
But the uphill battle isn't over yet
It's a battle for your soul
For your greatest adventure yet
The light is coming
It's on the horizon
Half cracked and half full, it all depends on your perspective
The illusion is breaking so you can become whole again
Even stronger than you were before
Your wings are blossoming and getting stronger every day
You are the light
You are the answer to every prayer you've ever had for more
More love
More life
More joy
More happiness
The answer is you

The energy of the mother flows through me.
I am her and she is me. I am one with the universe and all of its flow.
I am, I am, I am.
I am the divine and the divine is me.
I am a vessel for all of life's wonder.
We are meant to explore the beauty and the grace equally.
The human experience is a special one.
It is specific to each person, and each moment, and each melody of the soul.
Each soul is at a different frequency, yet we are all singing the same chorus.
We are all a unique sound in the universe's magic symphony.

———

All we have is each precious moment

As individual as dewdrops in spring or snowflakes in winter

Their permanence is fleeting

Just a few seconds of joy

Of love

Of laughter

And it's gone

Almost as if it never was

But the energetic vibration stays

Imprinted in our hearts

To remind us

That we lived

That we loved

That we had meaning beyond being stars floating in a vast void

Don't be afraid to take up space.
To walk tall.
To stand proud.
To speak your truth.

Rise to the day.
Rise to the spirit within you.
Even if there is sluggishness in your bones.
Rise.

Dive in and swim to the depths.
Be an explorer of your own soul visiting uncharted waters.
Go where you've never gone in this lifetime, in any lifetime.
What are you afraid of?
What you might find lurking at the bottom?
The forgotten sludge and silt of your soul?
The hidden secrets, shames, and desires?
Bring them to the light
For they are treasure. Each one.
There is gold in these buried memories and emotions.
Seek them.

You came to this planet for a unique purpose and journey
Part of that journey is a remembering
A knowing that on the soul level, you were meant for more than society tells you you are
Deeply
Feeling deeply
Giving deeply
Loving deeply
Some of us start our journeys in the deep end and then are told that's wrong, so we swim for the shallows
But the shallows aren't nourishing. They aren't where you're meant to be forever.
The shallows keep you small. Like a fish who quickly outgrows his tank.
Be a little fish in a big pond.

How can you soften?

It doesn't mean you're weak.

Actually the opposite.

So strong in yourself and your power nothing can shake you.

You can afford to show all sides of yourself because you are so YOU nothing can negatively affect you.

Come from a place of love and compassion no matter what.

Unwavering in your faith in yourself and who you are.

It doesn't matter what anyone else is doing or how you're perceived.

Closing off keeps you separate. It keeps you isolated and feeling bad. Our souls crave connection. Unity. No separation between ourselves and others. When it's hard, how can you open even more?

Crashing down all around me

The floodgates open

The tsunami arriving and making impact with the shore

My body just a vessel for all these too-big emotions

Too-big feelings

That I can't contain any longer

I can't hold back the tide

So I let go instead

Riding the waves of my surrender

Allowing the release

And just when I think it's done… there's more

Waiting to be unleashed

A torrential downpour of tears

Of fears

And shame and guilt

And everything I've locked inside

I am shattered to find I am still broken
Still broken
The second I take a breath, I am torn open
Torn open
On my knees, I pray, I cry, I beg
My head is so heavy
So heavy
Like I'll never hold it high again
Like a wave of sorrow will bow me forever
I kneel and my head is so heavy
The burden so full
I lay this burden at your feet
Will you help me carry it? Oh, god, please
How could I think the suffering was over?
It's still there. Buried deep
Like a stone in the middle of my chest
I wail and pound my fists
For what?
You're not coming back
For all this talk of letting go. I haven't, not really
You would have grown for three months today
My little jellybean
My little star
I feel like I'm drowning, I'm struggling against this never-ending weight upon my chest
I want out of this stupid house
Out of this stupid town where you died
Anywhere
I want to be anywhere but here
I thought this house would hold so much joy for us, only sorrow
Only sorrow lives here now

Please take it away
Take the pain away
Burn it from my soul so I may rise from the ashes again
Wash it all away until nothing but a smooth pebble remains
So smooth I can run my hands along the surface and not feel the cracks deep beneath

You are more than animated flesh and bone
Than rotting meat that's all alone
You are here for something more
That's stored within your DNA
Let this be an activation
As you awaken
From the deep slumber you've been under
Breathe life into your cells
Breathe life into your being
You've returned
Now rise.

I will not let this resentment ruin me.
I will not let this bitterness break me.
I will ask for what I need.
I will speak my truth.
I will share my disillusionment.
I will not stay quiet.
I will not stay small.
I will not just grin and bear it.
I am supported and I will act as such.
I control my thoughts, they do not control me.

I am salt and sand and sea,

tranquil as can be.

Anything your soul desires is possible. Believing is all it takes to make it real.

Everything you could ever want or imagine is right at the edge of your fingertips, waiting for you to take it.

Waiting for you to believe you deserve it.

Because you do.

You deserve everything your heart desires and more.

You deserve a joyful life. You deserve it all.

Stop telling yourself you don't.

And you sure as hell better stop letting other people tell you you don't, either.

Anything is possible. All you have to do is believe.

I'm tired of others' restrictions on me.
Of their thoughts.
Of their ideas.
Of their reality.
Allowing them to live rent-free.
I want to just be.
Free.
To be me.

What got you to where you are now might not be the thing that gets you to the next stage
With each new season, you become a different version of yourself
More of this, less of that
Let this season be one of softening
Of acceptance
Of carefree joy
Let go of who you once were to embrace who you're becoming
Get to know her day by day
Minute by minute
Hour by hour
Let her be different than you expected
Allow her to take shape without judgment
Shifting and changing without constraint
Trust what nourishes you and let her blossom
She is emerging

It's okay to be scared
It's okay to have butterflies before you make a big leap
Before you choose yourself
But never be scared you're making the wrong choice
Because you could never be wrong
Maybe misdirected
Maybe misinformed
But never wrong
Every twist and turn of your path allows you to go deeper
To learn more
To realign with love
And isn't that a beautiful gift?
To be reminded of your divinity every single day
To be reminded of what a miracle you are
And what a miracle it is YOU get to choose
What a gift
Choice is a gift. And we squander it by running in circles and not making that choice
By allowing our minds to get so twisted, we don't know which way is forward
But you know
You do
Deep down, you always know the path forward
You just may be too scared to take a step
That's okay
Then leap
With faith that the universe will catch you
With faith that you could never be wrong
With faith that you can say yes to re-aligning in every moment

I am the best medicine, and I honor what my body is telling me it needs.

So I decided to surrender and let the tidal wave come

What if it didn't have to look like you thought it had to look?

Just, any of it

The daily grind

The morning practice

The life

The car

The kids

What if it could be different?

Better?

But you had to take a leap. You had to have blind faith

Would you take it?

Would you grab the bull by the horns and just go for it?

Or would you settle for what's safe because it's what you've always done?

What they've always told you to do

Better to have some than none, right?

Meh, maybe not

Maybe you're just on the other side of THE BEST DAY OF YOUR LIFE

And you'll never know

Because you didn't take the leap

The path less traveled

The new route to work

The time to sit in stillness in the backyard

If you don't know, you won't miss it, right?

I'm not so sure

Even if you don't consciously know

Somewhere deep down, you do

You can't fool your soul

It was made for more

More than just going to work and coming home and watching tv until you die
That's not living
That's existing
But for what?
A paycheck you can't take with you
"Status" that doesn't really matter
A life unfulfilled isn't a life
No matter how much money you have in your bank account
Or how many instagram followers you have
It's hollow
It's fake
And it won't feed you, nourish you, the way your dreams do
So wake up and go for it
Wake up and do the damn thing
You weren't born to be mediocre
So stop acting like it
The world needs you in all of your glory
Not a sliver of your awareness because you're scared
You were made for more
Start acting like it

Don't be afraid of the dark, for it's where you'll find yourself
Embrace the unknown
You are the light
You have the power to face your fears and your demons
It starts with love
It starts with you
You are the love you seek
Go fully into the unknown

This world does not define you.
It can not contain you.
Make you shrink or be anything you're not.
You are limitless.
Full of infinite possibilities.
You are whole and perfect and lovely.
Emitting endless vibrations.
Full of love and abundance.
I see you.
I hear you.
I love you.

Allow the lows to guide you.
To see you through to the other side.
Let them be a lesson in even more surrender.
In even more grace.
In even more love.
You won't be here forever, darling.
Maybe not even tomorrow.
So wade your way through with patience and perseverance
For what is waiting for you on the other side is already yours.
And nobody can take it away from you.
Feel your inherent worthiness in your heart.
Deep in your bones.
And in your lows, allow them to buoy you.
To hold you.
To caress you.
For you still have the thing that matters most:
Hope.

You are all the elements, galaxies, stars, and planets combined.
You are a beautiful, multi-dimensional melting pot.
A wild force to be reckoned with.
The fire and power you have inside of you at this very moment are unparalleled.
Your spirit cannot be tamed.
You. Are. Unstoppable.

It feels as if I've fallen into an abyss
An in-between
In between who I am and who I'm meant to be
There is so much shedding and so much sorrow here
I'm in the empty in-between before my vessel is filled again
Like a boat floating listless in a storm
Waiting for the waves to come crashing down or the sun to come out again
It's agony
It's an unraveling
Of my consciousness at every level
Is it madness?
Maybe?
Is it real?
It's as if life is playing on a movie screen around me
The only time I feel alive is when my little boy is near or I'm outside looking at the clouds
Everything else makes me feel trapped, small
Like I'm biding time for something else
Someone else
Someway else
To swoop in and save me
To turn the lights back on at the station
Dust the cobwebs off and remind me to rise
But nobody is coming
I am the conductor
I am the lighthouse operator
I am the one who has to rise
I have to claw my way out
Or maybe I can float?
Maybe it can be gentle? Even if it doesn't feel gentle right now

I'm just so tired
I don't want to interact with the outside
I want to stay inside where it's quiet
Where it's cozy
Where only the sound of my heartbeat is what keeps me company
I'm not ready to emerge from the darkness just yet

What are you searching for?
What are you longing for?
What is this ache in your chest?

It's made from the mind
It's made from forgetting

Who you are.
And why you're here
And who you're meant to be in this moment

In every moment
You get to decide.

There is nothing to look for
She is already here
She is already yours to claim

Locked away behind a door you've kept her for so long
Your inner child
That inner little girl

You've wanted to keep her safe from the world
But what if instead you kept yourself safe from feeling
From being
From exploding into the very essence of you

She wants to be set free
Allow her to roam
It is safe
She is safe

You don't need to protect her from the world any longer
You never did

She is your very essence and she longs to explore
To love
To grow
To change
To evolve

So grab her hand and let her fly

Beautiful things are unfolding for you if you let them.
No matter where you are in your Earthly journey this incarnation, trust that you're exactly where you're meant to be.
Trust that you're divinely guided and supported.
Trust that the exact experiences you're going through are what you NEED to get you to your next destination.
Find peace for where you're at, while enjoying where you're going.
Trust your divine purpose.

There's a beauty in the in-between.

In the space before you really know. Or really let go.

The space of being unsure. Of being not enough. Of being too much.

The space in the middle is where the magic unfolds.

It's the mundane moments between the big things that drive life forward.

The pause between the spaces.

The hold between the inhale and exhale.

It's where anything can happen.

It's where everything happens.

There's beauty in the not knowing.

Because before you truly know, anything is possible.

Real change is messy... and I'm here for it.

Your next breakthrough is coming.

It's already on its way.

The next version of you is percolating, getting ready to emerge.

You've already seen glimpses of her in the day-to-day moments. It doesn't seem like much now, but I promise in a week from now, a month from now, a year from now, you'll hardly believe how far you've come.

Peel back the layers of your soul

Like a flower petal blooming

Nobody pushes a flower to bloom, it just does

On its own time

When it's meant to

So, bloom with intention

You choose when you bloom and for whom

It isn't for everyone

Not everyone deserves to see you at your brightest and fullest

Be careful of that energy

Of giving your energy to people and things that are not worthy of you and your time

Only you get to decide who is worthy

Your blooming is a precious gift

Treat it as such

It's not for everyone.

And you aren't meant to be blooming at all times

Look at nature

Everything blooms at its own time and in its own season

There is nothing that is ever-blooming

For the world doesn't work that way

You need time to go inward, to grow and sprout. For petals to die off and be replaced with new shiny ones. With new energy. With new growth.

Embrace both sides. Embrace the polarity within.

We're all just searching for love.

That fleeting feeling of joy deep in our chest. That pang when we know we're in the right place at the exact right time, feeling the fullest, boldest, biggest expression of ourselves that we can.

But they're all just fleeting, aren't they?

Any emotion.

Sadness, joy, grief, love.

None of them stay forever because we're meant to feel the FULL spectrum of emotions. All of them. Not just one.

And that polarity is what allows us to be human. Allows us to feel so deeply.

Out of the darkness comes the lotus.

Something is alchemizing and moving within me
The heavens and earth collide within my body
I am stardust and galaxies
I am heaven and earth
I am light and dark
I am a walking contradiction
I am everything and nothing
I am full and yet empty
I am divine and human
I am I am I am

I am solid and flowing
I am movement and stillness
I am grace and chaos
I am hard and soft
I am and I am not
I am the here and now

―――――――――

I am a vessel for your divine loving light

I am a sanctuary for your release

My body is a temple of creativity

The universe moves through me

Flow, flow, flow

The energy of creativity moves through my spirit

Spirit soars in my veins

I am merely a stopping point on the journey, but oh, what a beautiful stopping point.

I am but a vessel of ash and bones and flesh. From dust I come and so I will go

Until then, I serve no will but my own

Which is that of the universe because I am the universe

I am a vessel of stars shining from the inside out, beaming light upon us all.

I am a vessel.

Don't forget that you are a miracle.
Every day, every second is miraculous.
What a gift to live this life.
Truly live.
If you realized all that it took to get here.
All the ways in which things had to align and come together for your soul to be right here. Right now.
You wouldn't waste it.
You wouldn't spend another second doubting yourself.
Or ridiculing yourself.
Or doing anything but loving yourself fully.
You aren't meant to suffer eternally.
So don't stay there.
Don't stay in the sorrow.
Spread your wings and rise above your grief.
Impossible, you say.
Well, you said it right there — I'm possible.
Yes, you are.
And so is your ability to overcome.
This, too, shall pass.

Things are still unwinding in the slowness.
Movement happens whether YOU are moving or not.
Change comes no matter what.
You don't have to go out and greet it.
Settle in and let it come to you.
Be ready and waiting to receive.
Have the altar set.
The mood candles lit.
Make it the juiciest and yummiest expansion ever.
Honor the change so it can honor you.
Thank what you learned with ceremony.
And call in the new with gratitude.
It is no small thing to receive.
To be gifted a new perspective,
A new journey,
A new manifesto.
For that's all it is.
A chance to learn more,
Go deeper,
Go further,
And what a beautiful gift.

I'm so tired. I haven't stopped long enough to let things catch up.
My body,
My mind,
My weariness.
If I keep going, then nothing can get me, nothing can stop me. Nothing can hold me back. But I'm holding myself back.
From feeling. Fully.
From allowing the universe to flow through me.
It's like I've put a stopper in the top of my head to say, "No more, please."
But as I release, I make room.
As I let go, I receive more.
What am I afraid of?
An overflow of emotion?
It's going to be an avalanche if I don't let go soon.
It's going to be a tsunami that overtakes my body if I don't listen.
I'm so tired of carrying this weight.
This burden.
This heaviness.
And so today, I choose to let it go.
Back to the earth. Back to the heavens.
Back to all the people and places it belongs.
I call back myself.
MY power.
MY energy.
MY wholeness.
From all the things that have taken bites of me, like vultures picking at a carcass.
All the things that have worn me down with their needs, their wants, their unrepentant energy,
I breathe for me.

Into me.
Through me.

This world will run you down if you let it.
Don't.
Take your power back.

What would you do today if you knew you were 100% supported?

What would you say YES to?

What would you say no to?

What would you allow to effortlessly flow to you like running water in a stream?

You don't have to do anything.

Or be anything.

This support is unconditional.

It doesn't come with disclaimers or fine print.

This support is unwavering.

And already guaranteed.

You don't have to make a bargain or beg.

You just have to open your arms, and receive.

You were always held.

by the universe.

By yourself.

By the intrinsic wisdom of the world and your divine path.

Dripping of bees and honey

I can taste their sweetness on my lips

My tongue

In the entirety of my being

They come today to remind me to soften

To open

To bloom

To be the sweet nectar

To embrace the slow movement

To just be

Get it?

Bee.

You're arriving right on time.
You're not behind.
There's no hurry.
Things are unfolding exactly as they're meant to.
In perfect time.
It's divine.

We're always rushing to the next thing, the next opportunity, the next iteration of ourselves.
What if we just sat for a while in gratitude? In awe of what you already have.
There's this fascination with more, more, more.
But what you have is pretty great if you just take the time to look around and appreciate it.

BE HERE NOW.
Not future-tripping.
Not worrying about the past
Not worrying about anything.
The universe is conspiring in your favor.
Have faith and let it.
We always worry we need to be "doing" something.

You don't.
You don't need to do anything to receive.
To receive what is rightfully yours.

Why do we always want more than what we have, when what we have isn't so bad?

Today I choose happiness.

Today I choose light.

I feel you with me in this moment.
I hadn't felt you before.
Well, since you left.

It feels like I'm wearing a piece of myself outside my own body.
Like my heart is wrapped around my wrist and no longer beating in my chest.
Like my heart chakra is open and spilling into the world.
Spilling some of the sadness and heartache out so I can make room for love.
Nothing but love.

The windows to my soul are open and they're clearing the stagnant air.
The sadness.
Clearing out the chambers of my heart to make room for more love.
Nothing but love.

I am sad, but I know it's not forever.
I am tired, but I know it's not forever.
I am missing you, but I know it's not forever.

I know you'll be with me always,
With every breath I take and every step I walk
Hand in mine, always at my side

Near enough to talk to
To hold forever dear
To never forget.
I will break easily, only so I can mend the pieces back together

Better than new, sealed with gold.
I will spill tears only so the salt can cleanse my soul.
I will look upon the ocean and breathe deeper, letting salt and water replenish me.
Nothing is forever. But I'll be alright.

Aren't you tired?
Of trying to fit in.
Of trying to stand out.
Of trying to do all of the things society and others tell you that you should do?

What if you lived life just for you?
Solely and completely.
Following every whim and every desire you ever had. It wouldn't be bad.
To live from your heart instead of your mind.
To allow yourself the freedom to make ANY decision.

To follow any feeling.
To be exactly as you are.
Nothing more.
And nothing less.

I am woman, hear me roar!
I will not be silenced
I will not be put down
I will not be lessened
I will not be shunned
Or told what to do
I know what's best for myself and my body
Not you
Or you
Or you
I know what's best for the life growing inside of me
I know
And I will unleash fury upon anyone who doubts me
I will show them that they are wrong
I will show them my almighty power
I will expand and smite and smother anything that tries to stop me from expanding
From unleashing
From the reckoning that is me
From the hurricane that is my soul
From the words that are my sword
From the torrent of emotional downpour that's dripping out of my eyes
Out of my body
And out of my orifices
I am mighty
I am strong
I am capable
I am determined
I am fierce
I am unstoppable
I am a force to be reckoned with

Let your life be a constantly unfolding metamorphosis
A testament to change
To softness
To perseverance
To bending and not breaking
At least not completely

Allow yourself to unfold exactly as you're meant to
Releasing the ashes of forgotten lovers, feelings and resentments
Releasing
Releasing
Releasing

To begin anew and change. To truly change, first you must forget
Who you think you are
Who they taught you to be
Shedding the skin you've painted on layer by layer. Interaction by interaction over the years
Forgetting everything until you are nothing and no one other than who you're meant to be
Who you were born to be
Who you are at your very core
Your very essence
That glorious spark of light and love
Transcendent of any physical body
Or worry
Or shame
Just floating
Just being

Perfection has no place here.

If only you could see yourself through my eyes.
If you could see how powerful, and perfect, and protected you are.
That you are love in human form.
You are every single speck of magic and stardust that had to come together to create you.
You aren't a coincidence.
You aren't a mere happening.

If only you could know what deep love inspired your birth.
The love of the creator, the divine, the whole damn world.
Maybe you'd drink less.
Maybe you'd smile more.
Maybe you'd forgive yourself for all the mistakes you were meant to make.
Maybe you wouldn't take it all so seriously.
It's not like we get out alive anyway.

If only you'd let yourself take a chance, take the leap, travel into the unknown.
Let yourself be free, truly, and live from your heart.
Not from what anyone else wants of you, but from what YOU want. Deep down.

If only you believed as deeply as I do that you're destined for great things.
Naps and sunshine. Light reflecting off the back of butterfly wings, kisses under the moonlight and all of your wildest, most far-fetched dreams.

If only you could see yourself through my eyes.

Then maybe you'd know you are enough.
You are worthy.
And you are oh, so loved.

Today I release this unnecessary weight
This unnecessary pressure to be worthy
To live up to some ideal or expectation of myself
Whose expectation?
Mine?
Hah
Why do I put this pressure on myself?
Why do I feel like I have to be perfect all the time?
Where does it come from?
How do I rid myself of it?
Is it lifetimes of society weighing on my soul?
Is it my ancestors asking me to transmute their sadness and pain?
I don't want to
I don't want to do it anymore
I just want to be
Be free
And light
And happy
I'm tired of this weight of expectation
Of shame
And guilt
Of having to do and be someone I'm not
I want it to be okay to be a brat
I want it to be okay to be sad or mad or glad
Or happy
To just be whatever I'm feeling
And not have to answer to anyone or anything
And not have to give a fuck if I'm hurting someone's feelings
Or If I'm setting the wrong example
Or if I'm doing what I "shouldn't"

Fuck shouldn't
This pressure is too much
It's smothering
It's unfair
It's a weight I refuse to carry anymore.

What if we unbound ourselves?
Our feelings
Our emotions
Our joy
Our bigness

Unbind your powers, for that's what these things are
Your magic, your power, lies in the raw, unfiltered pieces of you

Stop apologizing for your presence
You deserve to walk tall, to take up room

Be your full, beautiful, bountiful, boundless, authentic self

You are sacred. It's time to start treating yourself as such.
You were meant to shine with the power of a thousand suns,
don't whisper with a small flicker of flame.

You don't have to be who they want you to be.
You don't have to think how they want you to think.
Being yourself is a beautiful act of rebellion. It's your own riot.
Your own stand in a world that wants you to be the same.
Be you. Be bright.
Don't give in to the ways of the world.
Stay strong in the faith of your heart and in the faith of your being.
You are more powerful and more worthy than you can ever imagine.
You are a walking manifestation of God.
You are creation in its most perfect form.
You are enough as you are.
Let anything else go.
Let it all crumble down.

Some days when I let the world in, I lose myself.
I let the anger rise.
The frustration build.
I don't want to give my energy away.
I don't want to interact.
I don't want to smile and play nice.
I just want to be left alone to cocoon in peace.
I want to be left to my own thoughts.
And dreams.
And wishes.
I'm so tired of the world pulling at me.
Taking pieces of me without my permission.
Poking into my energy field and taking what it wants.
On those days, I want to shut it all out.
I want to hide.
And it takes such a toll to pretend.
In fake conversations
With fake people
I'm done pretending.

It's time to rise.

Stand tall in your truth.

Stand tall in your power.

You are capable of absolutely anything.

Anything at all.

Unimaginable feats are your birthright.

Transcendence is calling your name.

With your feet firmly planted on the Earth, allow your heart to soar on eagle's wings.

Allow your consciousness to rise to new heights.

For when you are grounded, anything is possible.

Everything is possible.

Your energy is compounded with that of the earth, the sun, the moon, and the stars.

It is connected to everything and everyone around you.

Pulsing, vibrating, shimmering.

It is pure magic.

You are pure magic.

Breathe it all in.

Expand, expand, expand,

Soar beyond your wildest dreams.

Nothing is more urgent than your peace and happiness.

I can create anything I want.
I can BE anything I want.
I am an alchemist.
I am limitless.
I am divine.

Open your heart to new ways of being in the world
The uncomfortableness has a purpose
A reason
A peace
You are protected
Let yourself expand
Let yourself believe
Let yourself go there
There is nothing to be afraid of
You already hold the key to it all

———————

When I speak softly, I'm not heard
But when I'm louder, I am too loud
Too strident
Too forceful
I'm too much and never enough for you
Constantly tipping the scales one way or the other
Always holding my breath for the perfect balance
The magic frequency to make you actually see me
Actually open your eyes and take notice
It's a high-wire act I'm getting tired of
The shrinking
And expanding
And shrinking again
The constant pleasing and stifling and dimming
Enough I say
It's time I see me
It's time I speak to the sound of my own frequency

I am grateful for the uncomfortableness
I am grateful for the stickiness
I am grateful for these challenges and feelings
It means I am evolving
It means I am changing
I am not satisfied with the status quo
I am not satisfied with staying the same
I am reaching my edge — and then pushing past it
I choose overflow
I choose abundance
I feel more free
Thank you for the ability to shift
Thank you for this push

It's time to reclaim your power.

You are not helpless.

Break the chains of your oppression, your poverty, your inner feeling of worthlessness.

You are Shiva. Channel him and his mighty sword of destruction.

Let out a primal scream.

Have the courage to stand in your truth. To burn it all down. To be reborn.

To stand up not just for your beliefs, but for yourself.

Stop warring within yourself and bring that energy to the outside world.

We will rise.

Now is your time, sister.

Can you feel it?

You're releasing the shackles of lifetimes to ascend to new heights and dimensions.

If you've found this book, it's no coincidence. You are ready. Release fear, find forgiveness for yourself, and call the untamed goddess in each of us to rise and be set free.

The individual inner work you do isn't just for you: it's for your family. For your friends. And for the entire collective of human consciousness.

How are you showing up as the highest version of yourself each and every day?

You are a pillar of light, sister. Let it shine.

Universe, show me how good it gets.

The one thing I did right was become myself
Was become her
The woman I was always meant to be
The goddess I have always been
Unleashing her in full force upon the world
A hurricane and a balm equally
She is everything and nothing
I am her and she is you
The one thing I did right was remove the separation
Remove the "other"ness about myself
I am no better
I am no different
I am no martyr
I am divine
She is mine

It isn't always easy
God, it isn't always easy
But it's worth it
It's why I'm here
To lay myself bare
To strip myself so thoroughly of everything I thought I was
To open my heart and lean on others
To laugh together
To share
To let it go
To pass it on
To belong

The one thing I did right was listen
And surrender

And ask for more
More love
More light
More life
More of everything and not less
More is my birthright
More is nothing to be ashamed of
More isn't a dirty word, it's magic

The one thing I did right was love
And love wholeheartedly
Even when I gave pieces of myself away to those that were unworthy
But what is unworthy anyway
Everyone is worthy of something
Everyone deserves connection
And maybe everything I've done is right
Actually, I know it is
Every moment, every breath, every thought, every action
Nothing has ever been wrong

---

prompts & practices

Journaling

Journaling became such a sacred practice for me during this time of healing. I've always put pen to paper when I felt agitated or sad without really realizing why. Doing it intentionally allowed me to move through intense emotions with a little bit more grace. I hope these prompts allow you to do the same.

There is no right or wrong way to follow this section of the book. You can sit and write answers to them all, you can choose a question a day, you can go in chronological order, or you can skip around. Follow your intuition and your heart. They'll know exactly what medicine you need in the moment.

1. What do I love about my life right now?
2. Make a gratitude list. Write all the things you're thankful for in this moment — nothing is too small to acknowledge.
3. Getting out of my head and into my heart today looks like:
4. Who do I want to be in this moment? How do I want to feel?
5. How can I show myself more grace today?
6. Where do I feel tightness in my body?
7. Write a letter to your inner child today. What are all the things you wish someone else would say

to you right now? Say them to the little girl inside.
8. How can I nourish myself today?
9. Where in my life am I not showing up for myself fully?
10. Today, I am thankful for:
11. Peach & Pit: Peach is one sweet thing that happened to you today, and a Pit is one not-so-great thing. This practice helps you acknowledge both sides of whatever you're feeling.
12. If I could do anything with my life, it would be:
13. Here are all the sad words inside of me put to paper:
14. Today, I release:
15. Today, I plant seeds for:

Affirmations

Affirmations are another tool of encouragement you can use daily to raise your vibration and move through any sticky feelings. Some of my favorites are highlighted throughout the book, but you can create affirmations for yourself each morning. I wanted the affirmations included in the book to be works of art in and of themselves, so you could rip them out and put them on your mirror, or place them somewhere in your home you look at every day.

You can also just come back to reading them again and again, like I prefer to do. There's no right or wrong way to work with affirmations. You're literally affirming, or saying yes, to the things that you want more of in your life. You may not believe them fully just yet, and that's okay, but the more you work with them, the more they become true for you.

Two of my favorites:
Everything is working out in my favor.
The more I rest, the more I receive.

You can also create your own affirmations with I AM statements. I AM (insert how you want to feel that day/what you want to attract). Although affirmations are used to counteract a negative emotion, include positive words only, please.

Some examples: I AM free. I AM limitless. I AM embodying my highest self.
I AM bountiful. I AM blissful. I AM beautiful.
I AM a miracle.

Akashic Prayer

As I mentioned earlier, the Akashic Records are an energetic frequency and higher perspective you can tap into anytime you need love and support from the universe. "Akasha" means "totality of all," and the Akashic Records contain everything that has happened, can happen, or will happen, in your lifetime.

The Akashic Records are not a physical thing, but rather a universal energy hosted in the Pleiades (a star cluster). Each person has their own record, or frequency, that is housed in the Akashic Records, and the guardians of the Akashic Records are always beaming love, light, and wisdom to you.

When you open the Akashic Records, you are channeling the cosmic guidance you need in the moment. It is so much more than just a "reading" or divine guidance — it is a tuning of your energy. Yes, the exact guidance you need to hear in the moment is what comes through, but you're also tapping into a universal energy that is vast and expansive, while also the tiniest speck in the totality of the universe.

You can physically feel the energy, and the messages are truly a transmission of joy and love. This line of energy goes from your crown chakra straight to the stars. I like to think of that line of energy like strings on a guitar. When you open your Records, you're plucking your particular string to play the music of your heart, and realign with the magic that is already inside of you. It's tuning the guitar string of your energy and bringing it back to its divine nature.

I get asked a lot if the records are like fortune telling. No, the records aren't predicting the future, and sometimes they don't like to share the past — especially if it isn't going to add to your present.

I opened my Records in 2020 to have them explain, in their own words, what they are. Here is a snippet of that transmission:

Welcome, child. We welcome you with open arms.

The Akashic is for anyone and everyone. *It does not see boundaries or skin color or race or size. It is the infinite possibility of the universe. It is everything and nothing all at the same time. It is and it is not. You are and you are not. This is a sacred place to love and learn and grow and live. Our guidance isn't final and it isn't gospel or fated. What it is, is **just what you need to know, exactly when you need to know it.** We boost you up and are here to offer otherworldly wisdom when you need it most. Sometimes we're just here to fill you up with love and light and fairy dust (whatever fairy dust is to you).*

Our words are often simple, and the words of your father's father and mother's mother, of your ancient lineage and line that came from the primordial ooze. We are specks of stardust and ascendant masters. We are the universe, and the universe is us. Sometimes, we'll tell you the name of your spiritual watcher on the other side. Sometimes, we'll share your spirit animal or guide or even the color chakra you need to work on for inner love and peace and tranquility and paradise.

Don't take anything we say too seriously. It's not meant that way. We hope you leave each reading just feeling the infinite love and so blessed to be upon the Earthly plane. Some of us were on the Earthly plane once. Others were not. You can usually tell by the type of wisdom we provide. **You can access us anytime, and we are always there for you.** *We love listening to your prayers and your wishes, and we do our best to help you reach them.*

You have to do your part, too — free will and all that — but we are here to help you. Anytime. Rain or shine, day or night. Whether you believe in us or not. We are here, and that's beautiful. We are here. We are here. We are here. We hope you turn to us often. But it's okay if you don't. It's okay if you don't believe. We aren't here to try and make you a believer. We are here just for you. Just for your love and light, and to help you with this orbit around the sun.

You didn't always start on this planet. I guess we should tell you some of us aren't from this planet either. But that's okay. The more, the merrier, right? **We will never try to steer you in the** *wrong direction, and only want what's best for you and for those that you love. Our wisdom is not earth-shattering. It is often things you already know deep down inside that you're afraid to face. We help you face them. Together. We are always here with you. Always always always. You have more strength than you know, and we hope that you find it after chatting with us.*

Victoria is our conduit, and she will share the messages we find most pertinent to you in the moment. Sometimes we won't share everything with her because she is just a human being. Human beings aren't supposed to have all the answers. That's part of the beauty of being in an Earthly body. To experience life, and learn and grow, and not know what's coming next, or who, or what is just around the corner waiting for you. The divine and the beautiful. We hope you see the beauty of the world after and always. We're happy to remind you when you forget. For there is always something beautiful to be had.

Some quick tips:
- Come with an open heart.
- Open the Records with a question in mind.
- Frame your questions like, "How would it feel if…" or "How do I…" You have free will, so the Records will never tell you what you should or shouldn't do if you phrase a question that way.
- Move your body before you sit down to connect. Opening your heart through dance, yoga, walking, stretching, etc., before you channel

makes the transition to a high vibrational state much easier.

- This prayer and practice is meant for you only. Please don't open the Records for other people — especially those under 18. Too many karmic implications.
- You can, however, ask about someone else through your Record. For example, "How can I relate to my husband more during this vulnerable time?"
- Sometimes you won't hear anything at all, and that's okay. Just being in the energy of the Records is calming and cleansing.
- Sometimes the silence you receive is the answer. You're only meant to receive the guidance you need in the moment, and you may not need to know anything about that particular subject right now. For example, I asked the Records about my past lives multiple times before they shared anything because it wasn't relevant to me to know (even though I really wanted to know).
- Have fun. It's serious, but not. The more you realize the answers you're going to get don't have to mean anything if you don't want them to, you're free to receive exactly what you need.
- It can take some practice, but embracing the words of the prayer below with an open heart will automatically raise your vibration enough to connect with the frequency of the Akashic

Records. I like to free-write as a means of sharing messages. Don't think, and just let the pen flow across the page. You can also open the Voice Memo app on your phone and speak the words that bubble up inside of you.

Find a quiet spot and repeat this prayer three times to open your specific Akashic Record.

God/Goddess, support me in coming into an elevated, expanded state of consciousness.

Support me in becoming the clearest vessel for your divine loving guidance and knowing.

Allow me to set aside my earthly vibration and ascend my consciousness to one of clarity, purity, and love.

*Allow me to see myself at my highest vibration from Akashic perspective.

*Enable me to know myself as I am known in the light of the oneness of all.

*Let me clearly share the knowledge of my ascended masters, teachers, and loved ones for the highest good of myself and all involved.

[Repeat the starred lines 2x more silently to yourself]

I am love, I am love, I am love.

I am light, I am light, I am light.

I am, I am, I am.

And so it is.

The Records are now open.

Once you are finished, close your Records by thanking the ascended masters and teachers for their guidance. Asking that it all be integrated with ease and grace. Knowing that a seed has been planted in your heart for your highest good and the highest good of all involved. Visualize your energy coming back down from the stars, descending into your crown chakra, and all the way to the bottoms of your feet. As your body fills with energy, like a cup filling with water, allow yourself to feel heavy, grounding your energy back on the Earthly plane. Once you're completely full, put a stopper into your crown chakra and cut any last energy with imaginary scissors.

Then repeat the following three times:
The Records are now closed, amen.
The Records are now closed, amen.
The Records are now closed, amen.

Oracle Cards

To connect to my intuition daily, I lean on spiritual tools like oracle cards to help guide me. My favorite deck is one I created — *The Spirit Mamas Oracle* — but there are tons of oracle card decks out there. The key is to find one that speaks to your soul and work with it consistently.

I like to pick a card first thing in the morning by asking my guides and angels what I need to know for that day, or what guidance they'd like me to have. If I have time, I like to sit and journal afterward. It can help set the tone for your day and remind you that you're not alone on this journey.

Breathwork

Connecting to your breath is an easy, free resource I use to calm my nervous system quickly. You don't have to do anything fancy — just place one palm on your chest and one on your stomach as you take full belly breaths in through the nose and out through the mouth. Allow yourself to breathe as slowly and intentionally as possible. Instructions for my favorite breath sequences can be found below, or visit spiritmamas.com/breathexercises for short how-to videos.

Exercise 1: Breath of Fire

This breath is one that allows you to expand and increase your energy quickly. Please do not attempt this breathwork if you are pregnant. Sitting with your spine straight, chin gently tucked, and legs crossed, begin by filling the lungs 3/4 of the way full. Then, forcefully exhale out of the nose, pumping the navel toward the back of the spine. Allow the belly to expand as you inhale, and continue to contract as you exhale. Focus on the exhale, and the inhale will happen naturally. Start with 60 pumps, increasing your speed and intensity until you reach 120. I promise it gets easier over time. Once you've reached your final exhale, allow your breathing to return to normal on its own. Taking note of how your body feels different after this practice. Placing your hands/palms down on your thighs for grounding or facing them upward to receive. You can continue to sit in stillness, lie down, or go about your day.

Exercise 2: Fists of Anger

This breath is one that I honestly wish I'd found sooner. It's allowed me to move through deep, heavy emotions with grace. To start, sit with your spine straight, chin gently tucked, and legs crossed either on the floor or with your feet firmly planted if you're in a chair. Tuck the thumbs across your palms, closing all four fingers over the thumb in a fist. Close your eyes and begin to inhale and exhale out of an "O" shaped mouth. The arms are going to begin backstroking one at a time from your navel up and over your head to the base of your skull. Allow the motion to be fluid as each arm comes up and back. Sit here for three minutes, breathing and moving your arms. Sending all of your anger to your balled fists. Letting it rise with each breath. Once the three minutes are complete, inhale through the mouth and thread your fingers together, reaching your connected palms to the sky. Imagine white, glowing light flowing down into your hands and body, cleansing everything around you. Exhale and repeat two more times.

Exercise 3: Inner Voice Connection

Inner Voice Connection is one of the subtlest but most profound breathworks I have experienced. You can have someone facilitate the experience for you like I've been trained to do, or you can practice on your own. Sitting in a comfortable position, you're just inhaling through the nose and exhaling audibly out of the mouth as slowly as possible. Continue breathing in and out until the body begins to soften. Then, ask your inner voice to make its presence known to you. Once it has, you can begin asking any questions you'd like. Just wait until you've fully exhaled to receive the answer. When we hold the breath, we're holding on to our thoughts.

Dancing

Move. Your. Body. Grief gets stuck when it has nowhere to go. With movement comes release. Let go of the negative, pent-up energy by putting on some music and just flowing. Some days you might scream along with emo rock, others you might move your hips to faster jams. It doesn't have to be long, and it doesn't have to make sense. It's for you, and nobody else. Close your eyes and truly dance like nobody is watching. Let your body make whatever shapes it wants to. Allow your arms and legs to say the things your mouth cannot. Literally shake that shit out. Flail about. Envision all of your negative thoughts and energy flicking off in little droplets like a dog shaking out its fur. Follow your intuition and keep moving until you feel a shift. And if you end up crying, know that that's okay too. Tears are medicine. You might actually feel more drained than when you started, but you're planting the seeds to feel good tomorrow. Remember, grief, and the lifting of it, is a long game. Some days you'll feel amazing after this practice, while others, you just want to crawl into the fetal position and go back to bed. Do what YOU need in the moment.

Grounding

Plant your feet upon the Earth. I don't care if it's in a little piece of grass and dirt outside your house in the city. We're electromagnetic beings, and we reset when we're in connection with the electric charge of the Earth. If you have more space, feel free to lie on the ground with your face towards the sky.

Connecting to Mother Gaia reconnects you to the oneness of all, allowing you to slow down and regulate your nervous system. Envision the energy of the Earth flowing up through the bottoms of your feet, into your legs, through your torso, filling the front and back of your heart space, into your throat, down your arms, and then out of the crown of your head. You can even ask the Earth if she'd like some of your energy, reversing the flow from the crown of your head back down. Continue inhaling and exhaling, feeling that circuit of energy flow through you into the Earth and back again. Repeat daily for best results.

Acknowledgments

Where do I even start? I wouldn't be here without the many people who have guided, loved, shared, supported, and nurtured me along the way.

Will, thank you for giving me our beautiful boys, and for always loving me exactly as I am.

Sebastian, thank you for making me a mama.

Rocky, thank you for coming Earthside again. I know it was you who I miscarried in 2018. Thank you for giving me the wake-up call I needed to walk my true life's path.

Deanna, Cass, Erin, and Kayla, thank you for being there when I needed you most.

Kathryn, Stephanie, Kristi, Tiffany, Patsi, Morgan, thank you for being my soul sisters in so many lifetimes. For seeing me, and for helping me blossom.

Meg, thank you for being my book doula, mentor, and personal cheerleader. You helped me realize what this book could really be.

Britt and Tara, thank you for following your dharma and creating Elevate the Globe. This book literally would not be here without it.

Granny, thank you for showing me that grief doesn't have to win, and for being a living example of what a woman can survive (and thrive) after when she leads with love.

Mom, thank you for always believing in me and being the first to support my endeavors wholeheartedly. Your unconditional love shows me how to give my boys the same.

About the Author

Victoria is a trained Akashic Records Reader, certified inner voice & breathwork facilitator, and mama of two boys, Sebastian & Rocky. A miscarriage in 2018 rocked her world and kickstarted her spiritual journey. Learning to tap into her intuition through the Akashic Records helped heal her grief, and it ultimately overflowed into so much joy and love in her life. Accessing Akashic perspective has been profoundly healing for both Victoria and her clients, and she helps women all over the world learn how to access their own Records for daily guidance. Her personal mission is to help new and old mamas everywhere find the love for themselves that they have for their babies. Her website is spiritmamas.com.

Victoria is currently taking a limited number of 1:1 clients for 4-, 6-, and 12-month personalized experiences utilizing the tools in this book. Email info@spiritmamas.com to inquire.

STAY CONNECTED
Spiritmamas.com
instagram.com/spirit.mamas
tiktok.com/spirit.mamas

www.ingramcontent.com/pod-product-compliance
Lightning Source LLC
Chambersburg PA
CBHW072056110526
44590CB00018B/3198